JiG Fishing
For
STEELHEAD • SALMON and other SPECIES

Jim Bradbury

FRANK AMATO PUBLICATIONS
Portland, Oregon

DEDICATION:

To my wife, Joyce, who lets me go fishing everyday.
Thank you Honey.

ISBN: 1-878175-12-2

Front and Back Cover Photographs: Mike Henley
Book Design and Illustrations: Tony Amato
Typesetting: Charlie Clifford

Printed in U.S.A.

Contents:

ACKNOWLEDGEMENTS:

Thanks go to Hallie Jensen for typing and editing my original manuscript. Without her help this book would not have been completed for at least another year.

I would also like to thank my jig tiers. Without their help there would be little reason for this book. Thanks ladies.

ABOUT THE AUTHOR:

As a boy Jim Bradbury fished the Mississippi River and its backwaters for bluegill, bass, crappie, catfish, northern pike and walleye. During this period he used mostly spinners, plugs and bait. In 1968 his father-in-law taught him how to fly fish for bluegill and bass. From 1972 until he moved to Oregon in the spring of 1980, he lived in Michigan and Wisconsin and fished for salmon and steelhead.

His first year in Oregon was spent pursuing the mighty Columbia River sturgeon. During this time he and his wife, Joyce, took up residence in Eagle Creek, Oregon near Estacada and the Clackamas River. In the spring of 1982 Jim started fly fishing the upper Clackamas River for summer steelhead. From 1983 through 1984 he tied flies for Estacada Pet and Tackle. He has been an active member of the Association of Northwest Steelheaders since he moved to Eagle Creek.

In the spring of 1983 he tied his first steelhead jigs. They worked so well that Jim started selling them. Now there are two sizes (1/8th and 3/8th ounce), nearly 20 colors and combinations, and Jim employs three full-time tiers. The Bradbury Jig and bubble method is becoming widely know as one of the most productive methods for taking steelhead and other species.

Legendary jig fisherman Jim Bradbury caught this summer-run steelhead at the mouth of the Roaring River, a tributary to the Clackamas River.

INTRODUCTION:

I met Jim Bradbury a few years ago at the International Sportsman's Exposition in Portland, Oregon. He was telling anyone who would listen (and quite a few were) about how his jigs hook lots of summer steelhead on the upper Clackamas River–a stream about an hour away from Portland. With nothing more than a spinning rod and reel, six-pound test, bobber and jig, Jim said it was possible to sometimes hook as many as 15 summer steelhead per day. I had fished the upper Clackamas that past summer on numerous occasions, and at best I had hooked three fish in one day with spinners. I couldn't believe that an over-sized crappie jig would work better than spinners or bait. We talked about getting together, but nothing materialized.

One day during July of the next year I was driving along the upper Clackamas River when I noticed about

Nick Amato plays a feisty summer-run steelhead below River Mill Dam on the Clackamas River. With the aid of a 12-foot-long spinning rod the center of the river was easily reached.

12 anglers fishing with jigs and bobbers. I figured Jim must be in the area so I went down to the river and asked one of the bobber fishermen if he knew Jim Bradbury. He told me that he was a member of the Association of Northwest Steelheaders and that Jim was teaching chapter members how to jig and bobber fish. I found Jim downriver and asked him if I could tag along.

He asked me if I would like to catch a steelhead on a jig and I replied that I would love to. I followed Jim along with the chapter members to the next run. Jim let me use his setup, which looked more suited to trout, then showed me where to cast. Within five seconds my bobber went under. Honestly! A fresh summer-run steelhead hooked itself and proceeded to tear line off Jim's reel at an unbelievable rate. I just stood there, dumbfounded. The line then caught on the reel's bail causing it to break just above the purple and pink jig. Still in shock, I could hardly move. Anyone who fishes for steelhead knows that this kind of fast action just doesn't happen. Needless to say, I was sold.

Before noon, on that very sunny July day, I hooked four more steelhead and landed two of them – all on a red jig. Since that time I have never gone longer than about eight hours without hooking a steelhead when using the Bradbury Jig. (Of course I do have the advantage of knowing where many of the fish-holding spots are on the several different rivers I fish the most.) I've hooked winter and summer steelhead, and even spring Chinook. There is no question in my mind that when fished properly the jig and bobber method is one of the most effective ways to take steelhead. For beginners I can honestly say I think it is the best method. Read the following pages carefully, fish thoroughly (over fish), move frequently, put in the hours and I guarantee your steelhead catch rate (especially summer steelhead) will increase greatly. See you on the river.

– Nick Amato
Editor, *Salmon Trout Steelheader* magazine

PREFACE
WHAT IS A MARABOU JIG

It's alive! Originally marabou feathers came from the marabou stork, which lives in Africa, until it was nearly made extinct. Today marabou comes from turkeys.

I use the softest, longest feathers I can buy. These feathers are 3 1/2 to 4 inches long with no stem or quill, or backbone if you will. This means the slightest breeze, or in this case, the slightest current, will drive marabou feathers crazy, making them look **alive** to the fish.

The slightest current will cause the marabou jig to twist and turn. A light breeze on the water will make little ripples, causing the marabou to pulsate if suspended under a bubble (bobber), again making the jig look **alive.**

In rivers, as the current pulls on the jig, its feathers will slim down and the jig will rise. When the current lets up, the jig will drop down and the marabou feathers will open up, making the marabou jig look **alive.**

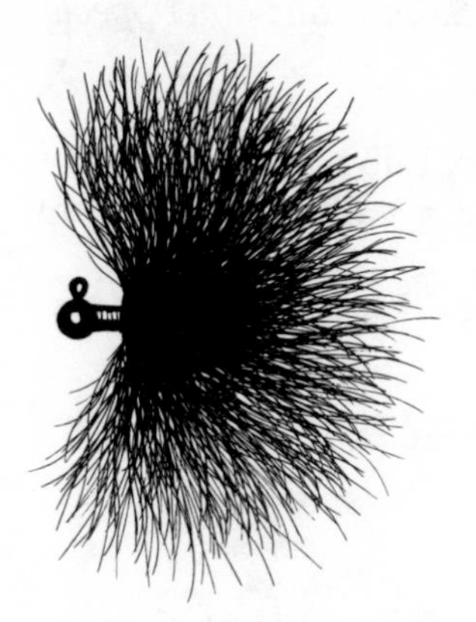

1

MARABOU JIG COLORS

All the pretty colors are not meant to catch fishermen's eyes but to help them catch fish. There are 10 individual colors and 11 combinations for different conditions.

Black – Black/Red; Black/Pink; Black/Chartreuse
Red – Red/Pink; Red/White; Red/Yellow
Purple – Purple/Pink
Pink – Pink/White
Orange – Orange/Yellow; Orange/Brown
White – Blue/White
Yellow
Chartreuse

COLOR REPRESENTATIONS

Black represents a leech or baby lamprey eel. It works best from June through December. Leeches hibernate in winter so black does not work well at this time. It's the same story with the brown/orange combination because crawfish also hibernate in winter. Crawfish and leeches are normally found in slow pools, so these representations should not be used in fast, riffly water or rapids.

Observing that nearly everything that lives in the water (minnows, frogs, stoneflies, crawfish...) is two-toned in color, I started tying two-tone colored jigs and have had greater success since doing so.

Black/red

Basically, this is a leech color. I do not know what it is supposed to represent, maybe a worm. But it is my first choice for summer fishing.

Black/pink

This one works best in fall between September and December.

Black/chartreuse

Works well for trout all summer and for fall coho.

Red

If you think this is the color of fish eggs, you are probably right. But remember there are no fish laying eggs from June through early September. This leads me to believe that something in the ocean that they feed on is reddish in color, thus making it a good producer all year long.

Red/pink

If you think red represents fish eggs then red and pink should represent fish eggs with a skein attached. It's my second choice as a year-round producer.

Red/white

Same thing as the other reds, except you will find that on some rivers the red/white, red/pink or red/yellow combinations will consistently take fish...and once the word gets out, that will be the hot color for that river.

Red/yellow

I do not know why, but from September through June it works very well.

Purple

To me it represents a squid. Of course there is no such creature as a freshwater squid, but in the ocean fish chase and eat them. You should not use purple in slow water, where fish can get a good look at it. Used in fast water purple looks and acts more like the real thing (a squid). It is a good choice for rivers with sandy bottoms, especially if the water is low and clear. It also works well in rivers with dark colored bottoms.

Purple/pink

I do not know what it represents, but it is my first choice for sandy river bottoms, or if the water is low and clear, which generally occurs in the summer.

Pink

If pink represents fish eggs then it's a good choice to use on sandy colored river bottoms. I have also had good success throughout the summer on dark colored bottoms.

Pink/white

My first choice on sunny days, over sandy colored river bottoms or in low, clear water throughout summer.

Orange

Another egg color. A good color to use when coho are in because it represents their eggs.

Orange/yellow

I am not sure what it represents, but I know when to use it – early in the year, January to June. I have a feeling it might resemble a sand shrimp. If you happen to fish below a half dozen fellows using sand shrimp for bait, get out your orange/yellow jig. Those fellows tend to lose their bait regularly, creating a fake sand shrimp hatch – a killer situation. But remember, your jig must drift naturally.

Brown/orange

Brown/orange is the color of crawfish, and it works well in slow, dead water from June through September.

It's not often beat. Occasionally I give it a try in winter, and sometimes a fish will fall for it.

Yellow

You have got me. I do not have the slightest idea what it resembles, but it works from January through June. It's on the top of my list if the water is up a little and moving.

Chartreuse

I am sorry but this is another effective color for which I do not have a reason. It works well for winter steelhead, winter coho and fall Chinook. Perhaps it represents a food item found in saltwater.

White

It must look like a minnow's belly. It works off and on all year. I particularly like it in the spring when nothing else seems to work. That is when it produces best for bass and walleye–I think for them that it's the best on the menu.

Blue/white

Ah! You are going to love this one. In salmon and steelhead streams during much of the late fall, winter and spring, fish are laying eggs. Come August, these eggs have produced two- to three-inch long juveniles. From August through December, it is tough to beat this color combination. The fish hit it hard, and keep on running–a blast to fish!

PAINT ON THE LEAD HEAD OF JIGS

I wish I had not painted the head when I started making jigs. I just imitated what was around at the time. I painted all the heads to match the main color of the body. As I fished, I would knock most of the paint off. Being lazy, I did not repaint them. I quickly realized it was not the paint fish were attracted to. Now the only reason I paint the head of the jig is to make them look pretty when you buy them. Don't expect the paint to stay on the head of the jig for more than 10 casts.

HOW TO KEEP THE COLORS FROM BLEEDING TOGETHER

When you change colors, squeeze all the excess water from the jig. Then put it in a pocket to air dry. This allows them to dry fast. The colors will not bleed and the hook won't rust. Don't put them in a plastic container until they are dry and fluffy again.

HOW TO CHOOSE YOUR STARTING COLOR

Remember, with this technique you are trying to match what fish would naturally eat – the jig has to blend in. What they feed on is usually camouflaged – living in moss, under rocks, or in schools like minnows do.

The secret is this – the darker it is around you (early morning, late evening, overcast days and dirty water), the darker the color jig you should use. And as the day lightens up, lighten up the color. In the early morning lighten your jig color and then stay with the color you are using about 8 a.m. for the rest of the day unless you see a fish rise, roll, flash or splash. At that point change colors several times to see if it wants something else.

I have learned over the years that if the river has a dark green bottom, the black colors work best early and late in the day, and red colors work best when it gets lighter. Over a sandy or light colored bottom, try purple first and then pink later. But when the water gets low and clear, purple or pink work well on dark colored bottoms. If the water turns dirty and the river has a sandy colored bottom, black or red work well.

2

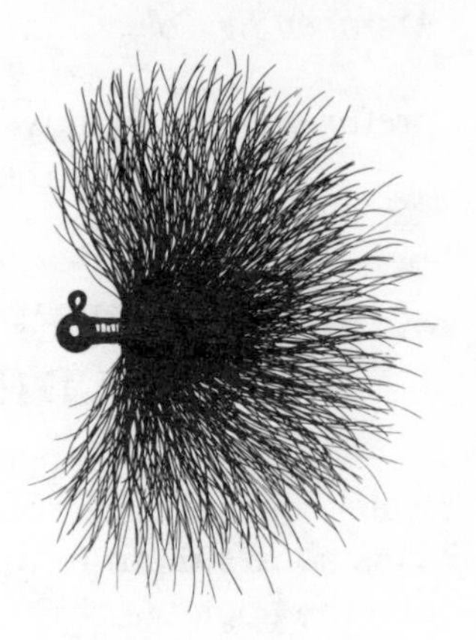

EQUIPMENT

WHAT BUBBLE TO USE

I use a Cast-a-Bubble which comes in different sizes; 1 1/2 inch and 3 inch work best. The larger size is used in any water type with 1/8- or 3/8-ounce jigs, and the smaller sized bubble is best used with the 1/8-ounce jig during low, clear water conditions or on small streams. I

One of five steelhead (in one morning) caught by Nick Amato on the upper Clackamas River in July. Red was the hot color on this particular day.

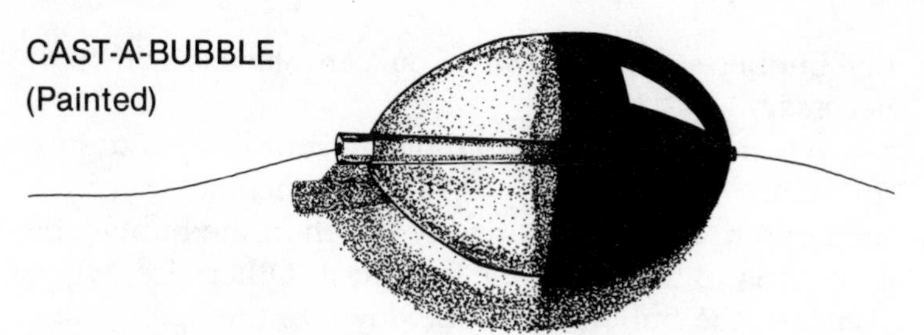

use the 3 inch bubble and 1/8-ounce jig 99 percent of the time.

The bubble is used to control depth. Use a hollow bubble that can be filled with water for casting weight. A 3-inch bubble half full of water weighs 1 ounce which is enough weight to cast a long way. Because the bubbles are made of clear plastic, normally you can not see them on the water. Paint half the bubble so you can see it. Do not paint it white, because then it will look like the foam and natural water bubbles already in the water and you will lose track of it at 25 yards. I paint the top half of my bubbles by first placing a dozen in an old egg carton and then spraying them with yellow or chartreuse/green paint. It takes only seconds and they are dry in 20 minutes.

Do not use red or orange paint because during summer, when you are fishing only a couple of feet deep, fish will sometimes come to the surface and take it! Orange is the worst color to paint the bubble. I had one fish hit an orange bubble four times on the same drift – hard evidence that orange is a very good color to use in summer.

The bubble has a tapered stem through its center. If you push down on the skinny end of the stem it will drop down but not come out, allowing you to hold the bubble underwater to fill it without losing the stem – I fill it halfway. Push the stem back in, and the water will stay in until you break the bubble which can happen if you hit it too hard on the rocks.

Because more than one company manufactures bubbles, the hole through the center of the stem is not always the same size. Normally I use a wood match for my bubble stop; that way you can shave it down if necessary.

When you thread the bubble on your line make sure the skinny end is up, so you can stick the match in from the bottom. Before sticking the match in the bubble, be sure to wrap the main line around it. Otherwise, when you cast, the bubble will slide down to the jig.

The match has to stick out from the bottom of the bubble, because when you cast, centrifugal force causes the bubble and jig to spin as it travels through the air. If the match stick is on top it is much easier for the line below the bubble to get tangled with the main line and the match, and if a fish hits your jig, the line can break and you can kiss that beauty good-bye.

ROD I LIKE TO USE

I like an eight and a half foot rod with a light to medium action tip. Recently I have been using rods up to 12 feet in length; the reason for the long rod is better line control. But remember, I have caught hundreds of steelhead on shorter rods and they are perfectly fine.

REEL I LIKE TO USE

I like to use a spinning reel with a line capacity of 180 yards of eight-pound test monofilament. Most of the time you will be retrieving line without tension as it drifts back downstream, thus it is best to use the softest line you can purchase because it will kink less than stiffer monofilament. I prefer Ande Tournament line.

LEVEL-WIND REELS

If you use a level-wind reel don't worry because all the fishing techniques are the same, its just that you will have a little trouble feeding out line on long drifts because some level-winds do not release line freely enough (this can cause the bubble to skate on the water). Also, you will only be able to achieve long casts by using the larger size bubble which outweighs the jig enough to pull it through the air, thus eliminating back lashes.

Betsy Leedy, member of the McLoughin Chapter of the Association of Northwest Steelheaders, proves that fishing for steelhead is not just a "man's sport."

3

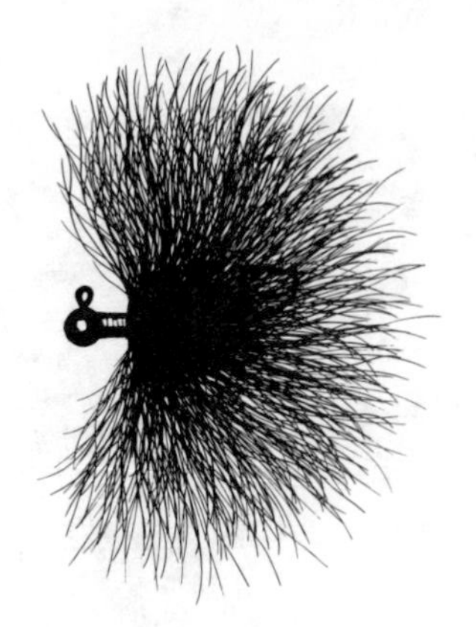

SUMMER STEELHEAD

HOW TO FISH FOR SUMMER STEELHEAD

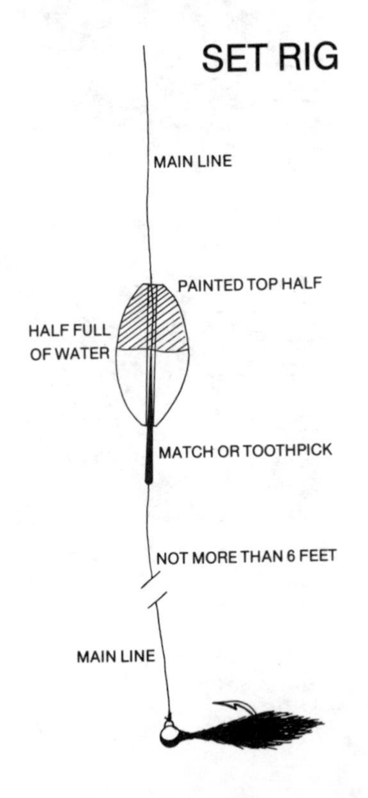

All you need to do is look at the section of water you want to fish. You should be able to at least faintly see rocks on the bottom, or maybe a shelf or submerged ledge. Set the distance of the jig from the bubble about half the distance from the surface of the water to the bottom of the river, or the structure to be fished. Obviously you have to estimate the water's depth.

I rarely fish more than two feet deep for summer steelhead(the distance from the bubble to the jig), and I like to fish water in which I can see bottom. I do not

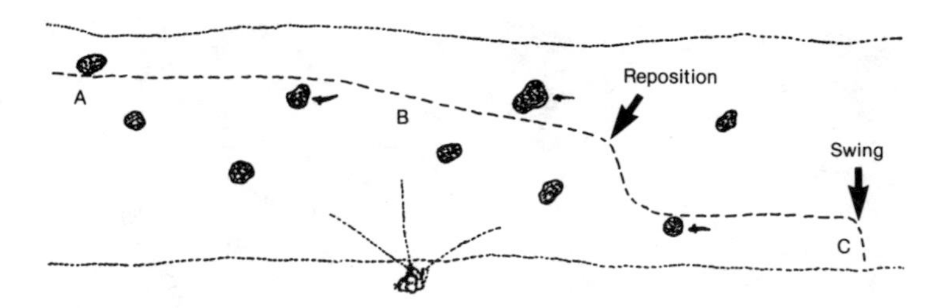

To fish effectively the bubble must drift "drag free" between points A and C. It is okay to "drag" the bubble across the surface briefly to reposition.

A. Keep your rod tip high and retrieve line to keep up slack so you can set the hook quickly. When a fish takes, strike hard!

B. As soon as the bubble reaches this point start free-spooling. Let the bubble drift without tension—except when repositioning to cover a slot. When a fish takes strike upstream with your rod low to the water.

C. Stop free-spooling and allow the setup to swing to the bank. Don't strike on the swing. Let the fish hook itself.

---

have to see every little pebble, but I want to know approximately how deep the water is. It is important to have swirly surface, so the fish can not see me. I also like lots of rocks, basketball size or bigger, to break the current and give fish a place to rest and watch for drifting food.

The object is to cast upstream, above the rock that you think the fish is hiding behind. (Do not cast to the area behind the rock or you will spook the fish.) As the bobber and jig drift downstream you retrieve line with your reel to eliminate slack so you can set the hook quickly and forcefully if a fish takes the jig.

Do not reel the bubble and jig downstream faster than the natural water flow. Fish will **not** hit if the bubble and jig are moving downstream faster than the current! Remember, you have to set the hook yourself; there should be no slack line. Once the bubble is directly across stream from your casting position start free-

Larry Ferguson, owner of the Barton Store, wrote the first article on the Bradbury Jig. It was published in *Salmon Trout Steelheader* magazine. He poses here with a summer-run steelhead.

spooling to allow the bobber and jig to cover more of the drift (see diagram).

Sometimes I am happily surprised by hooking a fish in a location I have never hooked one in before. If you do not hook a fish behind the rock you thought looked good, keep making casts three to four feet apart, until all the water you can reach is covered.

As your casts start reaching farther across stream, the greater the chance you have of the fish hooking itself. When your line is more across than upstream, then due to the fact that all the stream's flow is not moving at the same speed, you'll have to raise your rod to keep the belly out of your line. I repeat: fish will **not** hit if the current is dragging the bubble and jig downstream. Once the bubble is pulled under by a fish the current will instantly start dragging on all the line plus the bubble, and about 50 percent of the time the fish will hook itself.

If you had a hit up to this point **you did not feel the fish hit** (you only saw your bubble dip) because of the slack in the line created by the downstream drift. At the end of your drift, the bubble and jig are on the other side of the river, your line is tight between the rod tip and the bubble and the jig is swinging behind. The jig will be a couple of inches below the surface depending on current speed. Hold your rod high, keeping as much line off the water as you can. By holding your rod tip out over the water you can change the angle of the line between the rod tip and bubble allowing you to walk your bubble and jig across the heaviest rapids or shallowest water.

Your bubble will make a wake when dragged in the water, drawing the fish's attention (but if the jig is more than three or four feet from the bubble, the fish will

Jim Dunlap holds his first steelhead. The Bradbury jig can get anglers into steelhead fast.

chase down the bubble). Sometimes fish hit so hard they will even pull the stem completely out of the bubble, but 90 percent of the time, all you will feel is a **very** light tap–so light that you will be unsure you felt anything at all. If you strike when you feel that tap (which is the fish stopping the jig) most of the time you will miss, because everything is tight and the hook is facing away from the fish. But if you wait a second after the fish has the jig stopped, the current will continue to pull the bubble toward your bank, hooking the fish. **Do not strike on the swing.**

There is another trick I use when the bubble is making its swing; I manipulate the line and bubble, so that the bubble and jig will swing in behind a rock. Then I hold my rod tip up, keeping line off the water, causing the bubble and jig to hold in the slack water right behind the rock. Let the bubble sit there a minute or two, then drop your rod tip to the water directly downstream; this allows the current to grab your line, causing the bubble and jig to make a sudden dart to your side of the river. If a fish spots the jig making an escape, hang on, it will think your jig is a bait fish running for safety. The hit will jar your arm–clear down to your knees.

The bubble and jig technique is very productive. Most of the time if you get a hit it will be on the first or second cast, as your rig passes the rock a fish is resting behind.

I make three casts per rock: one on my side, one on the other side and one more in case the fish did not see it the first two times. If there is only one rock in a pool, three casts is all you get; go to the next hole. If there are 10 rocks in the hole and they are in a straight line, then you can cover them in three casts, that is all you need. If the rocks are staggered it is possible to cast to the top one and let the bubble and jig drift four feet past it, then reel in some line and let the rig drift by the next rock and so on. Three casts is all you get. **It is fast!**

Many different fish migrating upriver will hide behind the same rock in a particular hole if it offers them rest and sanctuary. If you catch a fish behind a rock **do not ever forget it!**, because if the fish are running in good numbers, there could be another fish behind that same rock in an hour. If not, there will probably be one there tomorrow. Many holding spots are good for many years until a flood changes the river.

MY FAVORITE SUMMER STEELHEAD STORY

A few years ago I took the members of the Sandy River Chapter of the Northwest Steelheaders out fishing. They landed a fair number of fish. I had one of the members stand on a rock and cast to a pocket in the river. Sure enough, he hooked and landed a fine summer steelhead – his first ever. He was extremely excited and wanted to show his wife his new-found fishing skills.

The next day, he took his wife to the same rock and five casts later she had landed two steelhead. She would not allow him to tag even one. They were both hers! Because she was limited out they had to stop fishing and go home.

On the way home she asked her husband in jest: How come you fish all the time and never bring any home? **What have you been doing?**

A member of Sandy River Chapter of the Association of Northwest Steelheaders jig fishes a classic run.

4

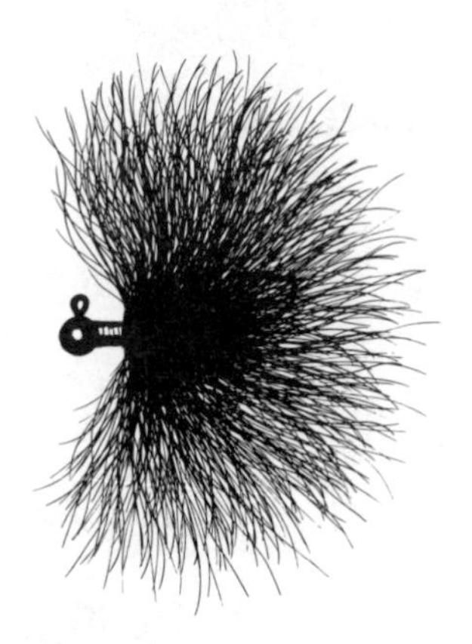

WINTER STEELHEAD

HOW TO RIG A ROD FOR WINTER STEELHEAD

In winter you have a different set of problems. The air and water are cold, and the fish's metabolism is slow which means they will not move very far or fast to take a lure. You have to look for the slowest and deepest water you can find.

You might even end up fishing 10 to 15 feet deep. I can tell you without a doubt that you cannot stand in the bushes or in a boat and dangle 10 or 12 feet of line (between your bubble and jig) from your rod tip and get a good cast. To solve this problem I use a sliding bubble set-up. Tie a swivel on one end of two feet of leader and a jig at the other end. Then tie a dacron (20-pound test) bubble stop knot onto the mainline. Below the bubble stop knot slide on a bead with a hole small enough so that the bubble stop will not be able to slide through it. Slide the bubble up your main line – small hole up. Now tie the main line to the swivel – be sure to use a swivel that is big enough not to get stuck in the bottom end of the bubble when you cast. Now you can slide your bubble stop up your line as far as you like, but when you cast, you will only be dangling two feet of line from the rod tip.

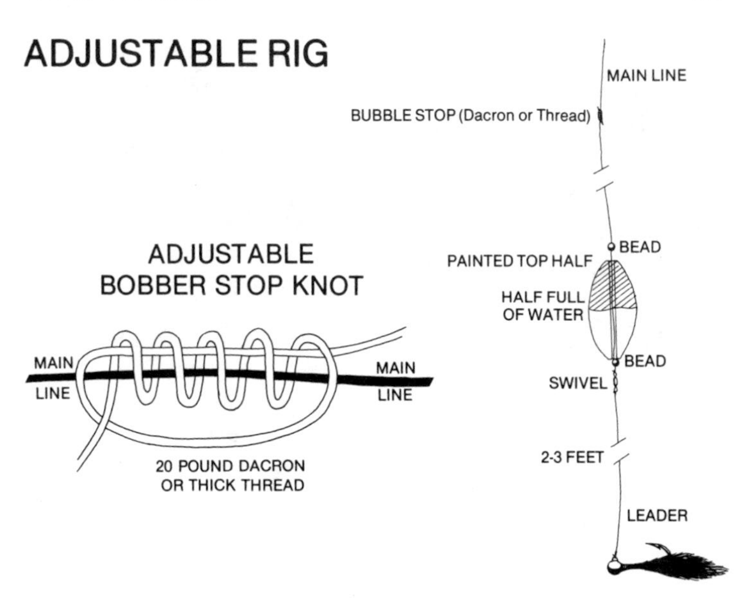

HOW TO FISH FOR WINTER STEELHEAD

Because you will be looking for the slowest and deepest water you should not be able to see bottom. The first step is to learn the bottom's contour. To start, set the bubble six feet from the jig. Cast upstream as far as you can. (Sometimes the current in these holes is so slow it might take the bubble and jig an hour to drift back. I do not have that much patience so I reel the bubble and jig downstream, but not fast enough to make the bubble wake—just a slow, steady retrieve.)

As it drifts back, reel in your slack. (The water might seem slow but the slack builds fast and can make it difficult to strike fish. You must be continually observant at reeling in slack line!) If the bubble does not dip it means that the jig has not touched bottom, so move the bubble stop up the line a couple of feet and cast again. The first time the bubble dips, reel in. (Do not wait for the second dip or you will probably lose the jig). Cast again two feet farther out and pay attention to where the bubble dips. You are attempting to discover where the bottom changes depth. It might be a straight line across the pool or diagonal or U shaped. You are looking for submerged boulders, slots and other structure. You might be able to make a straight drift at eight feet deep and then on the next cast, just two feet farther out, become snagged, and on the third cast two more feet out, the jig will pass freely. This means that you have found a submerged boulder or ledge. The next time you fish that hole, concentrate your fishing where you have found current obstructions and also where the bottom changes depth.

Because you can not be sure that there are fish at the bottom of these holes, change color a few times. Run one color on each drift until you cover all the water. Then switch to a lighter or darker color, depending on what color you fished first, and then cover all the water again. If you do not come up with a fish after six changes move on and **find another hole.**

Once you find bottom, move the bubble stop down two feet (this will raise the jig two feet). If the jig drifts

Slow, deep winter steelhead pool

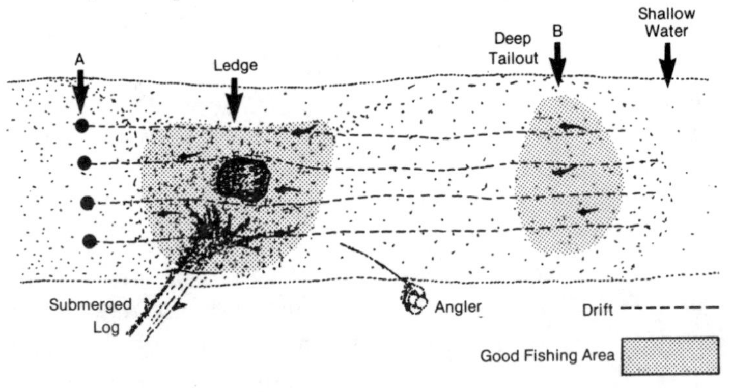

A. Make successive cast to this area. If necessary reel the bubble in slowly so that it doesn't make a wake. Start at six feet and go deeper on each cast until bottom structure is reached. Each time the bubble dips the jig has touched bottom—make a map. Use this knowledge to discover where fish are holding. At this point start changing colors.

B. End of Drift.

The author's fishing partner, Beverly Miller, displays a winter-run steelhead that she caught below River Mill Dam on the Clackamas River.

right into the fish's holding spot it will not have to move far to take it and might even reject the jig before you see the bubble dip (because the slow current will not pull the bubble down). If you make the fish come up and take the jig it will pull the bubble down when it drops back to its holding spot, and you will be alerted to the strike.

The strike is often in slow motion. You will see the bubble slowly sink out of sight, allowing plenty of time for you to make a couple of fast cranks on the reel handle to take up slack and set the hook with a tight line.

Not every run you fish is going to be 10 feet deep, and the fish do not get out and walk around the ones they do not like. So fish all the tailouts and behind big boulders. There is one place on the Sandy River where I only fish two feet deep in the winter. It is a long, flat run with many big rocks and the water is about three to four feet deep. It has been a constant producer.

If you are not sure if the water you are fishing in winter is slow enough, set the jig two to three feet from the bubble, make a short cast and watch the drift. If the jig trails behind the bubble at a 45 degree angle, the current is too fast for winter steelhead. **Fish slower water.**

MY FAVORITE WINTER STEELHEAD STORY

Actually, I have two special winter stories. My favorite took place at High Rocks, on the lower Clackamas River in December, a few years ago. Steve Kohler, a professional fishing guide, along with about 40 other fishermen, had been casting for two hours without raising a fish. I had given Steve a few jigs and he decided to tie on a red and pink one and in seven casts, he hooked five fish and landed four! (The water in this spot was eight feet deep.) A couple of days later, Larry's Sporting Goods was selling Bradbury Jigs.

My other favorite fish story occured in 1990. I hosted members of the Corvallis Chapter of the Northwest Steelheaders on December 27. We started fishing at 7:00 a.m. below River Mill Dam on the Clackamas and had not had a hit by 7:30 a.m., at which time I was ready to look for new water. It took another half hour to convince them they were not going to catch any fish here.

We then drove upstream to a Clackamas tributary. The first hole we fished on the Collawash River gave up two fish. Both were taken on pink and white jigs at a depth of four feet. The water was very low, and the river had frozen, then dropped – leaving a four-inch high shelf of ice along the bank, about six inches above the water. If the fish swam too close to the bank, the ice would cut the line, and as the fellows would walk out on the ice to meet the fish, the ice would brake and they would fall and then slide into the river!

To make a long story short they hooked eight fish and landed four. Three fell into the river and one fellow broke a rod. These were their first steelhead of the year and they wanted to go fishing again the next day. The rest of the fish that day were hooked on black/red or black/pink jigs between Two Rivers and Austin Hot Springs.

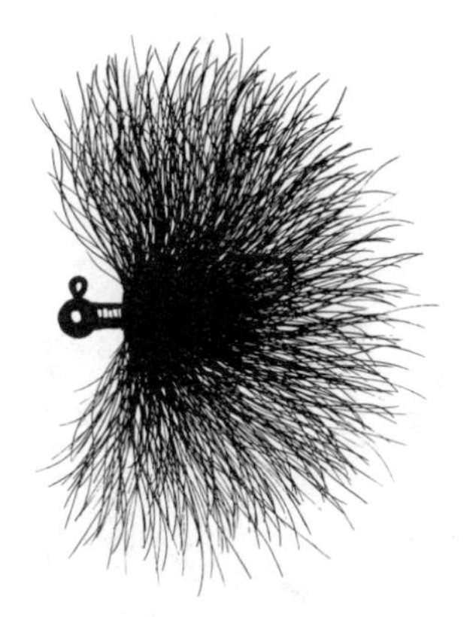

5

CHINOOK

The Clackamas River has two runs of Chinook, a strong spring run numbering five to eight thousand fish starting in early April and peaking in mid-May, and a much smaller fall run best fished in September.

There is a spring Chinook hatchery on the Clackamas River in McIver Park. Most of the river's hatchery fish return here and below the hatchery outlet good fishing can be experienced from mid-April through August. Several miles downstream is the mouth of Eagle Creek and in the past spring Chinook were also released from a hatchery located on it. The mouth of Eagle Creek still offers good fishing at times in May and June.

In June of 1986, as a member of the Northwest Steelheaders, I helped trap all the Chinook that made it up to the first ladder below Eagle Fern Park on Eagle Creek. We captured almost 500 fish and then trucked them up to Eagle Creek National Fish Hatchery where we dipped them in a green-colored chemical solution to prevent disease. After that we released them in cold spring water. Outwardly,strangely enough, they seemed to be in better shape in September, when we spawned them, then the day we caught them.

River Mill Dam represents a formidable obstacle to Chinook salmon, causing a major stacking of fish. There are days in May and June when 30 to 40 fish are caught

Jim Dunlap caught this mint-bright spring Chinook at the mouth of Eagle Creek with a black and red jig.

and lugged up the hill. Most fishermen use bobbers and bait.

I fish downstream from these fellows in water approximately eight feet deep and with a 3/8-ounce jig and 2/0 hook. When the bait fishermen cast they lose a lot of their bait, making this a very good area. Red and orange/yellow jigs work well because of the time of year and type of water. Black and brown/orange also work well. Over the years, I have learned that Chinook tend to like slow moving, deep running water and deep back eddies.

The Faraday Generator is located two miles upstream from River Mill Dam. Most of the Clackamas River is forced through the generator. Fish unsuccessfully attempt to swim up into the fast waters below the generator. The fish become confused and stack up (the channel of the river they need to navigate flows at less than 100 cubic feet of water per second). It takes them a long time to figure out which way to go.

The water in front of Faraday Generator is fairly shallow–don't fish more that five feet deep. Between

June 15 and November 1 there is a fishing deadline below the generator.

One mile upsteam, above some very slow water, is Cazadero Dam. Water in this area comes from the top of North Fork Reservior and in the late spring and on through summer it is very warm and the fish don't want to move up the one-mile-long fish ladder located here—causing yet another stack-up of spring Chinook salmon.

To correct this problem, on Tuesday nights in July, Portland General Electric Company releases cold water from the bottom of North Fork Reservior. This brings

Tom Sparks caught both of these spring Chinook in the Clackamas River with a pink and white jig.

the water flow in this area up to 500 cubic feet per second, causing Chinook to run upriver.

It's fun to watch what happens at 10:00 a.m. on Wednesday when they shut down the water flow. In about 15 minutes the water drops back to 100 cubic feet per second, causing the Chinook to go bananas. I have seen them trapped in water that did not even cover their backs.

An interesting thing I have noticed about salmon and steelhead is the fact that if a Chinook salmon moves into a pool with 10 steelhead in it, it will not be long before it owns the pool. In a large pool that has both Chinook and steelhead, the Chinook will be located at the head and the steelhead at the tail.

There is a fish trap in the ladder which is fed by North Fork Reservior, and spring Chinook salmon, along with summer steelhead, are trucked upsteam, which gives these steelhead a head start. I have caught summer steelhead at the mouth of Pinhead Creek, on June 4, 40 miles upstream from Estacada.

Don't forget to check the bubbles at Three Lynx during May, June, July and August (blue/white is a killer for Chinook in August and September).

In May of this past spring I jig-hooked over 30 Chinook in a three week period. After heavy spring rains the water flow in the Clackamas River rose to 5,000 cubic feet per second. (I had been catching quite a few summer steelhead on white, pink/white and yellow jigs while fishing three feet deep when the water was flowing at a more normal 2,000 cubic feet per second.) The water was way up into the trees and very dirty. Being a diehard fisherman, I had to give it a try anyway.

When I arrived, I could see a few fish rolling. Because the water was so brown, I started fishing six feet deep with a black jig. I stayed with this color for one-half hour and didn't get a hit. Next, I lowered my jig to eight feet and still could not find a biter. I switched to purple/pink to no avail. White had been working for summer runs so I tied one on. Still fishing at eight feet deep, the bobber went down immediately. I yanked hard on the rod, thinking I had snagged bottom. The line came tight but gave a little. Then, before I knew it, my reel's drag was singing–the fish was heading for the ocean. Ten minutes later I had a 12-pound Chinook laying on the bank. On my very next cast I landed another beauty.

That evening I called a few of my fishing buddies and related my experience. The next morning four friends and I limited out in less than three hours.

By the third day the water was clearing up a little, but the fishing was still great. I went for a personal record. On this particular day the fish seemed to prefer pink/white jigs over plain white ones. I hooked seven fish in the morning, left, came back at 3:00 p.m., and hooked seven more fish. As the water dropped and cleared we hooked fewer fish, and the fish hit different colors including blue/white, orange/yellow, red/pink and black. A week and a half later it rained heavily and the water came up and dirtied and the same great fishing occured again.

The author landed these two spring Chinook and lost at least eight more during one day. During a period of three weeks in May the author hooked over 30 springers.

6

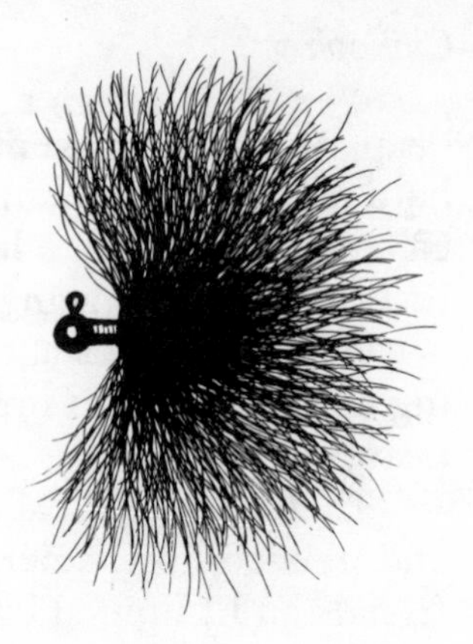

COHO

Coho are fun, aggressive bitters and good fighters. The Clackamas has two runs of coho. The early hatchery run starts during the middle of August and most of these fish are headed for Eagle Creek Hatchery. Because of the low water flow in Eagle Creek, below its entrance into the Clackamas is the prime spot to fish for them; they also like slow, deep water.

When I started hooking them it was with a dead drifted pink jig. Because there are summer steelhead in these pools at the same time, I would let the bubble and jig swing across the tailouts–at the end of the drift. It finally dawned on me that I was catching more than half my coho with that technique so I moved up into the deeper water that ranged from four to five feet in depth. By casting down and across stream and allowing the bubble and jig to swing across the current, my success rate jumped dramatically. I thought I had finally found the answer, but the best was still to come.

Because the coho were always rolling in the slow dead water, I thought it would be a good place to fish, but there was not enough current to make the bubble and jig swing at a good speed, so I started casting the 3/8 ounce jig without a bubble, letting it sink a couple of feet before starting a quick retrieve–not too fast for the fish to catch it and not slow enough to snag bottom. You would not believe how my catch rate jumped. The same technique works great for later running wild coho, too.

Joyce Bradbury, the author's wife, caught this fine coho in Eagle Creek during September.

During November the Clackamas has a winter run of wild coho. These fish like to hold in deeper water. Slow, dead drifting at depths of eight to ten feet is best and black and brown/orange work well. But this was kind of boring to me and I kept searching for another method.

I started casting the 3/8 ounce jig without a bubble. Guessing as to what the coho might like, I used a count down method, estimating that the 3/8 ounce jig would sink at a rate of about a foot per second. I would count it down to eight or ten feet and retrieve it fairly quickly and the fish seemed to like it that way. I assumed it worked because coho spend most of their life in the ocean chasing their prey. The best colors are black and brown/orange when dead drifted and white, purple and pink when retrieved.

In some areas I could see coho rolling in slow, dead water that was too shallow and rocky for the 3/8 ounce jig. I started using the bubble again, setting the depth of the jig so it would just clear the rocks. I would throw the bubble and jig upstream, then bring it back with a staccato retrieve. Make three or four fast cranks then briefly pause–continuing this retrieve all the way to the bank. (I have had coho hit while I was lifting the line, bubble and jig from the water. It shocks the heck out of you!)

Tom Sparks, member of the Clackamas River Chapter of the Association of Northwest Steelheaders, with a December coho that he caught below River Mill Dam.

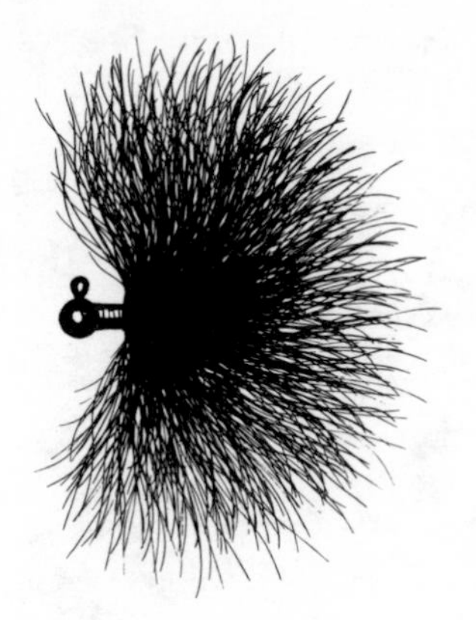

7

OTHER SPECIES

LAKE TROUT

I have not personally tried for this species yet, but I have had more than one fishing acquaintance tell me how they have caught fish using the jig. In spring, lake trout move into warm, shallow water about 20 to 30 feet deep.

Using a boat hopefully equipped with a fish finder, slowly troll until a school of fish is located. Using a marked line, let the jig down to the proper depth. Then **turn off the motor** and drift with the current, gently moving the jig up and down. If the wind is too strong or the fish are moving in the opposite direction of the drift, you will have to use a trolling motor to maintain correct fishing distance.

Because of the favorable reports I have received from friends, I am anxious to try this technique myself. **These fish are minnow eaters.**

WALLEYE

I do not pursue walleye and the few I do catch are taken while chasing bass. But there is one consistent factor – walleye eat minnows. If you fish locations where minnows and walleye hang out, you stand a good chance of catching walleye.

Jerry Marks of Duquesne, PA and five friends caught five walleyes apiece in Ohio with orange jigs.

Connecting lakes or other bodies of water along the Columbia River can be good producers. Water flows slowly between the river and "lake," providing minnows a safe haven and also a resting place out of the heavy current.

These ponds were created when truckloads of large rocks where dumped to create foundations for roads. The good part is that they used big rocks, giving the minnows plenty of places to hide.

Someone must have told the bass and walleye about the great smorgasbord. Coming from Illinois and having fished the Mississippi River for close to 30 years, I have caught many walleye near wing dams, islands and below locks. It makes sense that walleye like to patrol around rocks in order to capture minnows that hide near them.

I dislike losing jigs on the rocks so I use a bubble to control the depth of the jig. Because the depth is often more then four feet, I use the slip bubble technique – (see fishing for winter steelhead).

Most of the minnows I have watched do not swim erratically (like a jig worked quickly) unless they are being chased. Most of the time they sit motionless, with only an occasional twitch. I am not very patient, so I might let the jig sit for 30 or 40 seconds, then start retrieving just fast enough to cause the line to be pulled up through the bubble, causing the jig to rise. Then I pause a moment and let the weight of the jig pull it back down, creating a smoother swimming action. The best colors are white, chartreuse, blue/white and yellow, orange and purple/pink.

LARGEMOUTH BASS

Largemouth bass are relatively easy to catch in late spring and summer with crankbaits, spinnerbaits or plastic worms. But when they are hard to come by, particularly during early spring and late fall, I use my formerly secret technique. I cast the bubble and jig around downed trees, brush piles, wing dams, pilings or other underwater structures. I fish the jig at least a foot off the bottom and retrieve **very slowly.**

Minnow imitations work best during this time of year because it is either too late or too early in the season for leaches or crawfish. But if I have not fished a particular location before, and the minnow imitations are not working, I will try a leach imitation.

My favorite technique is to cast the bubble and jig into lily pads and retrieve **very slowly.** The bubble will slide around the lily pads causing the jig to appear as though it is swimming through the stems and it is very effective on large bass. This method also works exceptionally well on northern pike – yellow is a killer color.

SMALLMOUTH BASS

If smallmouth grew to the size and weight of steelhead, a tug of war between the two would probably end as a tie, with the smallmouth probably winning the acrobatics category. To hook smallmouth use the same techniques outlined in the summer steelhead section. Lean heavily on black, brown/orange, white, blue/white and yellow. There is probably no better minnow eating machine then the smallmouth bass. When fishing, pay particular attention to rocks or points of land that are rocky and have a good current.

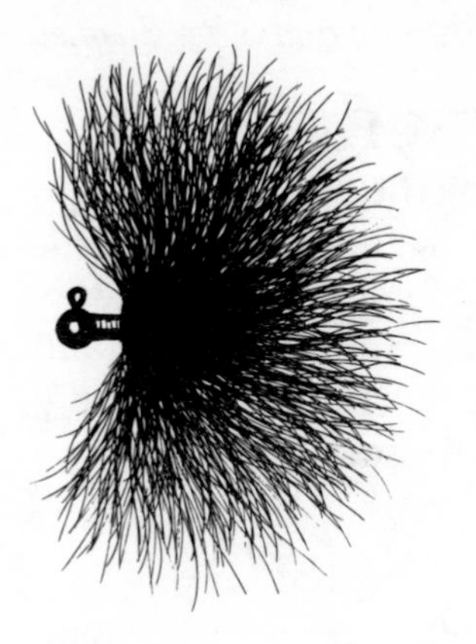

8

FISHING INFORMATION

SETTING THE HOOK ON LONG DRIFTS

Lets assume there is a spot downstream you would like to cover but can not reach on foot. Just open your bail and let the bubble and jig drift downstream. I really enjoy the challenge of seeing how far away I can hook a fish.

However, with this technique slack line becomes a problem. Your bubble and jig may be on the other side of the river, but when you open your bail, released line will create a long "J" shaped belly. This does not effect the way the bubble and jig drift, but it does make a difference on how you set the hook. If a fish hits when you have that much line out, and you try to set the hook by striking your rod straight up, most likely you will only yank the big belly out of your line and into the air, creating lots of slack and thus not hook the fish. But if you keep your rod tip down by the water, close to the bank and yank upstream, the current will catch your line, automatically setting the hook for you. Actually, you will be striking downstream because of the belly in the line, thus setting the hook into the back corner of the fish's mouth.

FISHING THE DESCHUTES

Another technique when using the 3/8 ounce jig is to cast it and let it drift downriver (without a bubble), as you would a spinner or spoon. I do not recommend this technique unless the water is at least five feet deep and has a good flow. This technique works as well as any other on the Deschutes. Black and purple are the two most popular colors followed by red.

WHERE TO FIND FISH

I do not consider myself an expert fisherman, however for many years I have taken the time to keep track of every fish I have caught. Draw a map in your log book, include mile marker, time of day, color of water, water height and time of year. When the river is high in the winter and spring, fish will hold behind rocks some of which might become totally exposed during the low flows of summer and fall. Sunlight will sometimes make a difference too, so keep track of whether your fish are caught in sunlight or shadows in different spots. If you want to have an opportunity to hook lots of fish find out where the fish are!

The best book I have read on the subject of discovering when and where steelhead are located (both winter and summer run) is *Western Steelhead Fishing Guide* by Milt Keizer. What makes this book so important is that in the back of the book Keizer has taken time to list every river in Oregon, Washington and British Columbia that has a government recorded steelhead catch rate, according to returned fishing tags for the 1985 fishing season. We know fish runs fluctuate from year to year, but this book gives you a month by month idea of how many fish were caught and kept. Simply look at the statistics on a monthly basis and then determine what river you want to try.

Now that you know which rivers you want to fish, where the heck are the fish? We are talking about summer run steelhead. On my river, the Clackamas, our summer runs start to show as early as March in some years, with the bulk of the run (about 4500 fish most